My Sabbath Walk

Phyllis Contreras

TEACH Services, Inc.
P U B L I S H I N G
www.TEACHServices.com ● (800) 367-1844

Copyright © 2014 Phyllis Contreras
Copyright © 2014 TEACH Services, Inc.
ISBN-13: 978-1-4796-0416-6 (Paperback)
ISBN-13: 978-1-4796-0417-3 (iPad Fixed)
ISBN-13: 978-1-4796-0418-0 (Kindle Fixed)
Library of Congress Control Number: 2014911045

TEACH Services, Inc.
PUBLISHING
www.TEACHServices.com ● (800) 367-1844

My Sabbath Walk

Phyllis Contreras

"Call the Sabbath a delight."
Isaiah 58:13

I like to go for a walk...

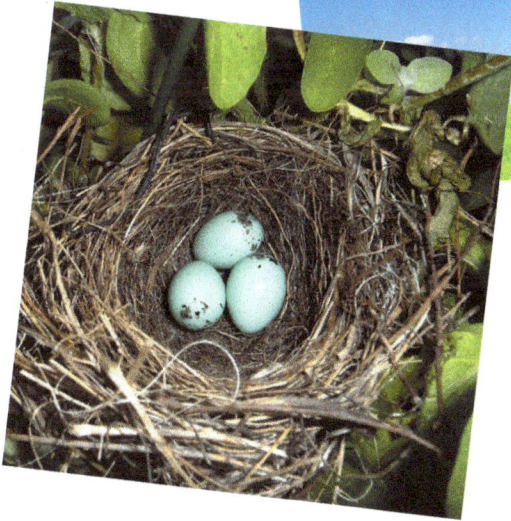

to see the things God made.

The pretty flowers smell so
sweet, and I know who made
the flowers...

God
did!

The tall trees have bark that feels rough, and I know who made the trees...

God
did!

I can hear the little birds singing, and I know who made the birds...

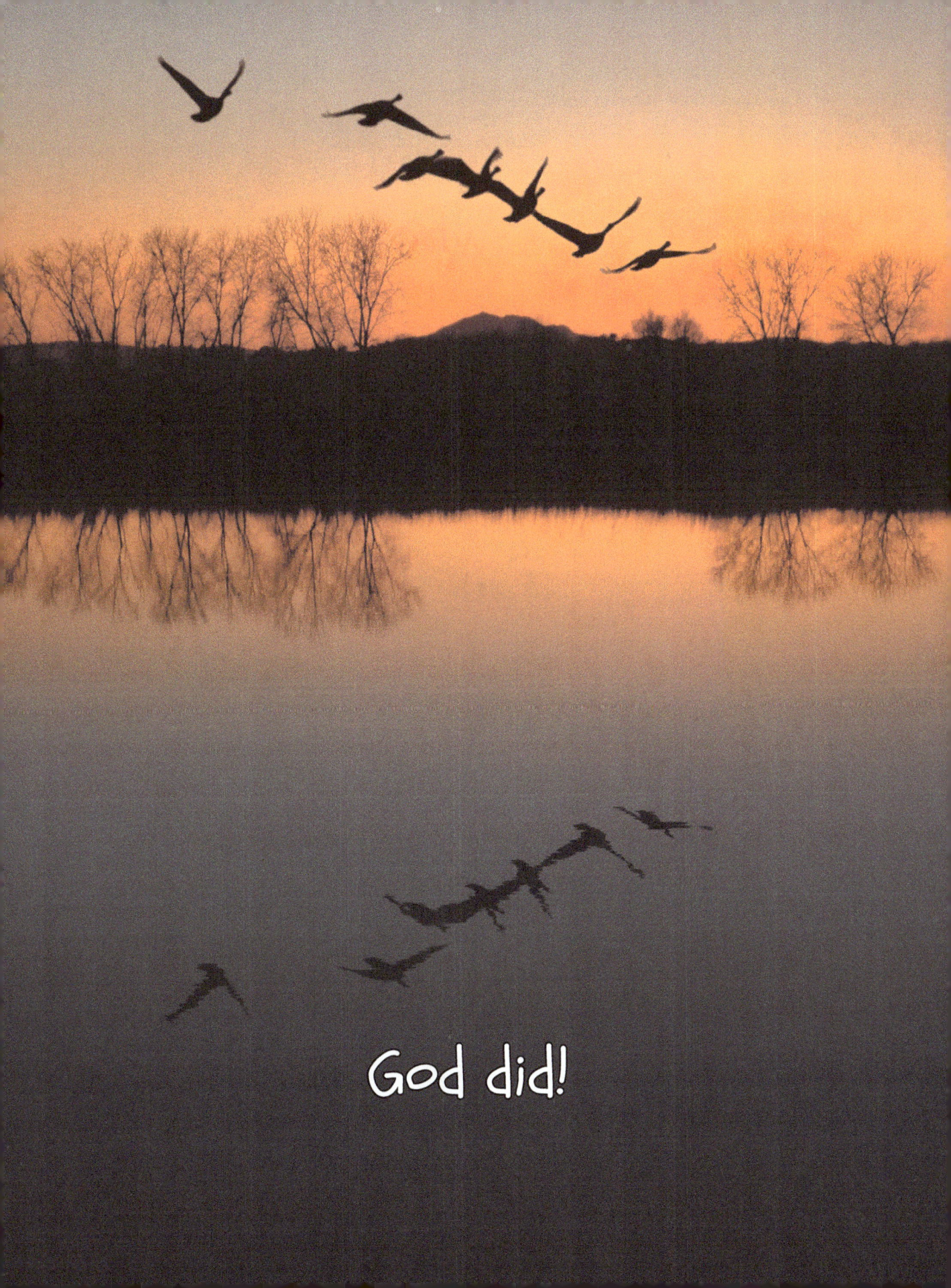

God did!

The white clouds look so fluffy
way up in the sky,
and I know who made the
clouds...

God did!

I like the taste of cool water after my Sabbath walk.

Do you know who made the water?

God
did!

Hmmm... Do you know what else God made?

Me!

(Parents: To personalize this page, encourage your child to look at his/her reflection in a mirror.)

We invite you to view the complete
selection of titles we publish at:

www.TEACHServices.com

Scan with your mobile
device to go directly
to our website.

Please write or e-mail us your praises, reactions, or
thoughts about this or any other book we publish at:

TEACH Services, Inc.
PUBLISHING
www.TEACHServices.com • (800) 367-1844

P.O. Box 954
Ringgold, GA 30736

info@TEACHServices.com

TEACH Services, Inc., titles may be purchased in bulk for
educational, business, fund-raising, or sales promotional use.
For information, please e-mail:

BulkSales@TEACHServices.com

Finally, if you are interested in seeing
your own book in print, please contact us at

publishing@TEACHServices.com

We would be happy to review your manuscript for free.

www.ingramcontent.com/pod-product-compliance
Lightning Source LLC
Chambersburg PA
CBHW080537090426
42733CB00015B/2610